KYOTO

by Yoshikazu Izumoji

translated by
Thomas I. Elliott

HOIKUSHA

THE HEART OF KYOTO

for YASE, KURAMA

for MT. HIEI

CONTENTS

JISHO-JI (SILVER PAVILION)

MT. DAIMONJI

KAZAKI
HOTEL

NANZEN-JI

MIYAKO HOTEL

for OTSU

TOKAIDO LINE

for TOKYO

for TOKYO

KYOTO

by Yoshikazu Izumoji

translated by Thomas I. Elliott & Don Kenny

© All rights reserved. No. 4 of Hoikusha's Color Books Series. Published by Hoikusha Publishing Co., Ltd., 17-13, 1-chome, Uemachi, Higashi-ku, Osaka, 540 Japan. ISBN 4-586-54004-4. First Edition in 1963. Thirty-third Edition in 1983. Printed in JAPAN

Looking east toward doll-like statue, Gojô Bridge and Higashiyama Mountains

KYOTO

Go where you will in Kyoto, nature is always right there in the background. Kyoto is also a city where the old and new blend together wonderfully.

Stand on Gojô Street, for example, looking east, and you see the Higashiyama Mountains in the background. Finial ornaments, rich in history, are seen on the modern Gojô Bridge. On Gojô Street, just below the bridge, there are doll-like statues of Benkei, the hero of all Japanese children. He remains unruffled amid the sounds of endless cars and trucks.

GION FESTIVAL

There was an epidemic in Kyoto at the end of the ninth century. Hoping to halt the spread of disease a shrine was dedicated at the eastern end of Shijô Street to the god Susano-o. This is Yasaka Shrine of today, known also as Gionsha. The belief that the epidemic long ago was halted through divine intercession has grown stronger over the centuries, and the Gion Festival, held to commemorate the event, has grown more colorful. Yamaboko floats in the festival procession were remodeled at the end of the sixteenth and beginning of the seventeenth centuries.

Gion Festival

2

Sanmon Gate of Tôfuku-ji

HIGASHIYAMA AREA

Tôfuku-ji is a Zen temple located at the western foot of Mt. E-nichi, the southernmost peak of the Higashiyama Mountains. It was founded in 1236 by Michiie Fujiwara and its seven halls make it a temple representative of the magnificant style of the old past. Both the great size and the name of the temple indicate how Tôfuku-ji was founded to vie with Tôdai-ji and Kôfuku-ji Temples in Nara.

Three works in Tôfuku-ji are designated Important Cultural Assets (hereafter abbreviated ICA). One is a painting done by Sesshû (1420–1506), one is the Zen Hall rebuilt in the fourteenth century, and the third is a washroom which accommodates three hundred and fifty persons.

The first abbot of Tôfuku-ji was Ben-nen, the first national priest of Japan. For a while, the temple ranked second among the five great Zen temples of Kyoto. After the time of Yoshimitsu Ashikaga (1358–1408), however, it dropped in rank to the fourth position. Sanmon Gate is a National Treasure (hereafter abbreviated NT), and dates from the beginning of the Muromachi Period (early fourteenth century). The gate copies the style of the Nandaimon Gate of Tôdai-ji Temple. The ceiling painting in the room of the gate is by the priest Minchô (1352–1431).

The view from Tsûten Bridge of the different structures in Tôfuku-ji is impressive. Viewed from Gekka Gate (ICA), a gift from the Emperor Kameyama (1249–1305), the moon rising above the eastern mountains is a beautiful sight.

Ryôgin, the abbot's chamber, dates from the early fourteenth century. It was here that the first abbot of Nanzen-ji Temple, Mukan Fumon who was a disciple of Ben-nen had his cell. Before leaving Tôfuku-ji it would be good to visit Fundain Temple in the compound to see the garden designed by Sesshû.

In Hôshô-ji Temple, off Honmachi Street, is preserved a Heian Period wooden statue of a thousand-handed Kan-non (NT). It is a splendid work in the emon honba style of sculpturing. The temple was founded by Tadahira Fujiwara, and this statue of the temple's deity has stood with its gentle expression since 924. Through it we can imagine also what kind of person Tadahira himself was.

Main Hall of Kiyomizu Temple (NT)

Overall view of Kiyomizu Temple ▶

The Main Hall of Kiyomizu Temple is for the adoration of Kannon. Familiar to every visitor to Kyoto is the famous Kiyomizu platform surrounding the Main Hall and the Prayer Hall of three sides. Two pictures, one each in the Prayer Hall and Okunoin, were gifts from traders at the time of the rebuilding of the temple in the Kan-ei Period (1624–1643).

Looking into Sennyû-ji
from Higashiyama Gate

Sennyû-ji Temple, holding special significance for the Imperial Household, is also known as Mitera. It was founded in 1220 by the priest Shunjô. The Emperor Shijô revered the priest and directed that his own grave be located here. When one stands in front of the gate taken here from the Imperial Palace by Nobunaga Oda and looks down the slope at the other structures — structures tied to the Tokugawa family, and to the Emperor Meiji — one cannot help feeling the Imperial quality of the temple.

Three deities are housed in the hall: Miroku, Shaka and Amida. They were prayed to for the happiness of the people of the country for three states of existence. North of the Reimyôden, the Hall of Spirits, are mausoleums and stone memorials for emperors and empresses all the way from the thirteenth century to the seventeenth century.

Were one to compare the gardens in front of the mausoleums here with the splendid memorial to the various shôgun of the Tokugawa family — Tôshôgû of Nikkô, for example — it would be seen that the feeling of purity and cleanliness here is much stronger.

Kan-non statues in Main Hall of Renge-ôin

Many potters live in the area between Sennyû-ji Temple and Higashi Ôji Street. As you leave the area look up the street on the western side. The giant comphor tree there will direct you to the compound of the Ima Kumano Shrine.

North from the shrines, after crossing the bridge over the Tôkaidô Line of National Railway, one passes the Municipal College of Fine Arts and Chishakuin Temple, mother temple of the Shingon Sect, on the right. Sanjûsangendô, the Main Hall of Renge-ôin Temple, is on the left.

The present Sanjûsangendô, dating from 1266, is a National Treasure, and its large sitting Kan-non (NT) is one of the last works of the sculptor Tankei (1173–1256). Altogether there are one thousand and one Kan-non statues in the hall. Except for one hundred and twenty attributed directly to Unkei (d. 1223), all are the works of Tankei and his disciples.

Maiko of Gion Quarter at the tea houses prospered in front of Gion Shrine. They are wearing traditionally long obi.

10

Five-storied pagoda of Hôkan-ji (Yasaka Pagoda)

Hôjû-ji in heart of Palace of retired Emperor Goshirakawa

Hideyoshi Toyotomi (1537–1598) founded Hôkô-ji and, mourning the death of his infant son Sutegimi, he also founded Shôun-ji Temple. Later, Hideyori rebuilt a Buddha statue in the temple in copper and gold, and constructed a mausoleum for his father, Hideyoshi. Misinterpretations of compositions for the bell in the temple led to the punishment of the composer, Bun-ei Seikan of Tôfuku-ji Temple, and led also to the ultimate downfall of the Toyotomi family. The memorial Hôkoku Shrine and Hideyoshi's grave were both destroyed. Ima-hie Shrine, which once stood on the grounds of the present Fine Arts College, was moved to replace the Hôkoku Shrine. There were changes also in the status of Myôhôin Temple which had sided with the Tokugawa family. It was elevated to the position of monzeki temple. That is, member of the Imperial family was installed as its head.

Chishakuin Temple, south of Myôhôin and across the old horse fair grounds, was given to Shôun-ji Temple by Ieyasu

Karamon Gate of Hôkoku Shrine

Tokugawa. On the sliding doors and the walls are many works in the National Treasure class ordered by Hideyoshi and executed by the Hasegawa School.

Yôgen-in Temple was erected in front of Sanjûsangendô by the wife of Hidetada Tokugawa (1579–1632) for her father, Nagamasa Asai. It was located in a spot which enabled it to watch over the temples in the area with ties to Toyotomi.

Hôjû-ji Temple of the Tendai Sect is dedicated to St. Shinran. A never ending flow of pilgrims pays homage here. Originally founded by Tamemitsu Fujiwara for the consort of the Emperor Kazan, Hôjû-ji once prospered as a monzeki temple.

The Karamon Gate of Hôkoku Shrine south of the bell of Hôkô-ji Temple was moved from Nanzen-ji by the Emperor Meiji when the shrine was rebuilt here. The bell had gone to Nanzen-ji from Nijô Castle, and to Nijô Castle from Fushimi Castle.

Chion-in prospered as the mother temple of the Jôdo Sect. The temple stands in tribute to Hônen, the founder of the sect. The Sanmon Gate (ICA), a gift from Hidetada Tokugawa, displays the glorious construction of the Zen style.

Sanmon Gate of Chion-in ▶

14

There are many people who wash themselves of worldly impurities in the cleanliness of the garden of Ken-nin-ji.

◀Garden of Ryôsokuin in Ken-nin-ji

Statue of St. Kûya
in Rokuharamitsu-ji

Obon, Buddhist memorial services, are observed in August in Kyoto. From Nishi Ôtani, the main mausoleum of Nishi Hongan-ji Temple, all the way down Gojô Street on both left and right are lined the homes and shops of Kyoto potters. The area gets busier and busier towards the final days of obon services as pottery merchants from all over the country gather in Kyoto. Vases and other pottery from here are used in services sending spirits off on their return trip to Higan, the other world.

Rokuharamitsu-ji Temple holds special significance being seventeenth among the thirty-three temples designated for special visiting. The temple was founded by St. Kûya (903-962), the first priest in Japan made a saint. St. Kûya travelled all over the country saving souls suffering from sicknesses.

Ken-nin-ji Temple of the Rinzai Sect of Zen Buddhism is northwest of here. At one time it was designated first among the five great zen temples in Kyoto. Initial prosperity was followed by a period of decay. It once again came into prosperity under Ben-nen, founder of Tôfuku-ji Temple. Famous in the temple is the abbot's chamber from Ankoku-ji Temple of Hiroshima Prefecture. The celebrated gods of wind and thunder by Sôtatsu (NT) are well worth a visit.

Yasaka Hôkan-ji Temple, rebuilt by Yoshimitsu Ashikaga in 1440, is located at the end of a narrow road leading east off Higashi Ôji Street. In the same general area are tea houses and other spots tied to the priest Saigyô and to the haiku poet Bashô. From nearby Chôraku-ji Temple, historically connected to the tragic Kenreimon-in, one passes northward through Maruyama Park to come out in front of the large bell of Chion-in.

It was in this area, given to Hônen and his disciple Shinran by Jien of Shôren-in Temple — a monzeki temple — that St. Hônen first began to preach the tenets of his Jôdo Sect. It was also here that another disciple of Hônen, Genchi by name, opened a hall — once a part of Shôren-in — that was to become the great Chion-in. The general area is called Ôtani, and the correct name for Chion-in is Ôtani-ji Temple. St. Shinran's mausoleum was once northwest of the temple but was moved at the beginning of the Edo Period. The area thus became divided into west and east Ôtani, Nishi Ôtani and Higashi Ôtani.

A great camphor tree north of the markers for Shinran's mausoleum and the mausoleum of the Emperor Hanazono is a guide to Shôren-in.

Camphor tree in Shôren-in

Heian Shrine from inside Main Gate

Heian Shrine was built in 1895, on the eleventh hundredth anniversary of the founding of Kyoto as the capital of Japan. Buildings in the shrine are copies of structures of Heian Kyoto (the eighth century to the twelfth century) on a scale of five to eight. Enshrined here are the spirits of the Emperors Kammu and Kômei.

Costumes and manners during the eleventh century when Kyoto was the capital are seen in the Festival of the Ages held in October by Heian Shrine.

◀ Festival of the Ages

The garden outside the abbot's chamber of Nanzen-ji Temple is the subject of some controversy. One group claims it as the work of the master gardener Enshû Kobori (1579–1647), while another feels it is from a later period, perhaps around Genroku (1688–1703). From the garden one may look towards the canal and see Nanzen-in, the former living quarters of the Emperor Kameyama. Works in the ICA class by Tan-yû and Naonobu Kanô, and by Tôhaku are in buildings near the Sanmon Gate.

Zenrin-ji Temple, north of Nanzen-ji, was founded by Eikan for the veneration of Amida Bodhisattva. It has been known popularly as Eikandô Temple since the latter part of the eleventh century. When the temple was founded there were many Buddhists who fawned on the aristocracy. As a lesson for these people, a statue of Nyorai was carved with the head turned as if looking back. Time should not be spent attending to the aristocracy, this statue emphasized, but used to save the common people. No similar image exists.

"Looking Back" Amida in Eikandô

Garden in Hônen-in

Sanmon Gate of Nanzen-in

Three-storied pagoda of Shin-nyodô

Eikandô was turned over to the Jôdo Sect after the death of Hônen in the early thirteenth century. Besides having treasures such as the "Looking Back" Nyorai and the Kamakura Period Mandara picture, Eikandô is also famous as a spot for viewing autumn colors and the young leaves of spring.

North from here, on the quiet road to Jishô-ji Temple, the Silver Pavilion, are found memorials to Anraku and Jûren. They were two priests beheaded by the Emperor Gotoba for accepting Matsumushi and Suzumushi, two girls of the court, into nunhood. Graves of the girls and the priests are said to be preserved in Anraku-ji Temple along here. Hônen-in Temple was the scene of this incident, which also resulted in Hônen being banished.

West from here, on Yoshida Hill, are found Yoshida Shrine of the Fujiwara family, and Daigengû Shrine where gods from the various provinces are enshrined. A famous services, Tsuina, held here in February drives away devils and evils for the coming year.

On the hill north of and connected to Yoshida is found Gokuraku-ji Temple (Shin-nyodô) of the Tendai Sect.

Northwest of Mt. Nyoigatake, at the foot of another small mountain is Ginkaku (the Silver Pavilion), Jishô-ji Temple. A fence is set high on a rock wall on either side of the path inside the front gate. That sight, and the sight of the garden inside the second gate, tugs at one's heart. A sand plateau, Ginshaden, serves as a moon viewing platform and sits between Ginkaku and Tôgûdô, both National Treasure. The garden is in the style of the Moss Temple garden with low, middle, and upper parts. Today, the middle garden has only partly been restored.

Ginkaku (Silver Pavilion) of Jishô-ji Temple ▶

View of pond and garden in Shugakuin Imperial Villa

Daimonji
bonfire

On the sixteenth of August, the last night of obon memorial services in Kyoto, fire is set to the giant character "dai" on the side of the Mt. Nyoigatake. After the closing of Japan to world trade in the seventeenth century, the merchants in the huge weaving area is surrounded on three sides, a dual purpose is served by the fires. They are prayers for the restoration of prosperity to Nishijin, and also guide the souls of the dead back to Higan.

Especially quiet, and possessing a fresh beauty, is Shisendô Temple, Jôzan Ichikawa, a former samurai of the Tokugawa family, built this as a hermitage. He lived here thirty years until his death in 1672 at the age of ninety. Jôzan collected paintings of thirty-six Chinese poets, Shisen. From that comes the name Shisendô, Poet's Hermitage.

After visiting Manjuin Temple of the Tendai Sect, at the southern edge of Shugakuin Imperial Villa, and the nearby nun's temple Rinkyû-ji, one passes through Yase and then starts into Ôhara. Ôhara is the beginning of Kyoto North.

KYOTO NORTH

Manjuin Temple was reestablished in 1656 in the northern part of the Ichijôji area by Prince Ryôshô. Since Ryôshô was the younger son of Prince Toshihito Hachijô-no-miya, the creator of Katsura Imperial Villa, the garden, shoin, and eight-windowed tea room here all demand special attention.

In the early seventeenth century, hoping to revive the power of the court, the Emperor Gomizuno-o conceived a bold plan to enlarge Kamo Shrine, and to recover its fiefs in some provinces. Additional rice payments from these fiefs, he reasoned, would eventually become Imperial wealth.

Although work began on the outside gardens of the Kamo Shrine, the central bakufu government realized what the Emperor was attempting and immediately ordered Chion-in Temple strengthened to meet any emergency. This, of course, ruined the Emperor's plan.

Following the Emperor's retirement, however, Ietsuna Tokugawa (1641–1680) ordered a portion of the original garden plan to be completed in just the way the Emperor desired. This is Shugakuin Imperial Villa of today. The pond of the upper tea pavilion, the splendour of the shrubbery, plants, and trees and the magnitude of the vista all speak for the large-mindedness of the Emperor.

Garden of Manjuin

On the fifteenth of May, Imperial messengers depart from the Old Palace in a procession that weaves through the streets of Kyoto to both the Lower and Upper Kamo Shrines.

From the hollyhock (aoi) pinned to the hair of the participants in the procession comes the name Aoi Festival. The exhibition and the procession are classical scrolls a thousand years old come to life.

Aoi Festival of Kamo Shrine

Amida statues (ICA) in Main Hall of Gokurakuin

Among the many historical and literary spots in Ôhara, Jakkôin Temple where Kenreimon-in lived after the defeat of the Taira family, and the mausoleum of the retired Emperor Gotoba and Juntoku are very famous. Main Hall (ICA) of Gokurakuin in the garden of Sanzen-in Temple in Ôhara sits low under cryptomeria trees.

Kyoto International Conference Hall

Garden of Sanzen-in in Ôhara   Oharame

Polular in Yase at the foot of Mt. Hiei is a type of bath said passed down from the time of the Kika, the naturalized Japanese who settled in the Kyoto area even before the founding of the capital in 794.

In the Heian Period the men of Yase always rushed to Kyoto to fight for the court when there was trouble. For their outstanding loyalty they held a special tax dispensation. At the time of Tsunayoshi Tokugawa (1646–1709), the dispensation was voided. A later investigation by Takatomo Akimoto resulted in the privilege being re-extended. To show their gratitude, the men of Yase initiated an annual pilgrimage to the shrine dedicated to Akimoto. This falls on the evening of the second of October. During the pilgrimage, male children perform a dance with flowers.

Sanzen-in Temple in the area was founded by St. Denkyô in the eighth century. In Gokurakuin, on either side of the sitting Amida (ICA), there are two guardian statues (ICA) which were given to the temple in 1148 by a woman known as Shin-nyobô.

Mt. Hiei through the garden of Entsû-ji

The platform the statues sit on is low, and the boat-shaped ceiling is topped by a low roof. It can be imagined that the overall consideration was to allow women and commoners to approach without fear as closely as possible. This contrasted with the strict aloofness in Enryaku-ji Temple on nearby Mt. Hiei.

Splotch-patterned kimono peculiar to Ôhara women known as Oharame, and said to be copied from clothes worn by the attendants of Kenreimon-in who stayed in Jakkôin are a charming sight when the women today come to Kyoto hawking various products.

Entsû-ji Temple in the upper Kamo area is a former mountain villa of the Emperor Gomizuno-o made into a temple of the Rinzai Sect. Moss in the garden, likened to the waves of the sea, is spotted with large and small rocks simulating islands. Far, far in the background, through high trees, is seen Mt. Hiei.

The Abbot's Chamber (NT) of Daisen-in in Daitoku-ji is ▶
the oldest of its type in existence (P. 31 above).

In Kôetsu-ji Temple, not too far from Daitoku-ji, is found ▲
the grave of Hon-ami Kôetsu, an artist and artisan of the early
Edo Period.

Gardens such as in Daisen-in, where mountains and water ▶
are expressed by rock and sand, are also observed in the
Chinese landscape paintings of the Yüan and Sung Dynasties.

Daitoku-ji Temple is a Rinzai Sect temple opened by the priest Daitô. Overcoming adversities and with the aid of many daimyô converts, Daitoku-ji grew in size and increased the number of their student priests.

Badly scarred in the Ônin Wars (1467—1477), Daitoku-ji was restored by the son of the Emperor Gokomatsu. The Abbot's Chamber of the time is preserved today as priest's living quarters (ICA). Momoyama architecture in the temple includes the Sanmon Gate, Butsuden, and Hattô (all ICA). On the ceilings inside the Sanmon Gate and the Hattô are dragons by Tôhaku. The early seventeenth century Abbot's Chamber (NT) has paintings by Tan-yû Kanô. The Karamon Gate (NT) was originally in Hideyoshi's mansion Jurakudai.

Other places of sightseeing interest are found in the subsidiary temples of Daitoku-ji. In Kohôan are tea pavilions and a garden done in the taste of the gardener Enshû Kobori. In Shinjuan are an Imperial Make-up Room, the tea pavilion Teigyokuken, and Tsûsen-in. Daisen-in, of course, boasts of

Bôsen Tea Room in Kohôan

its rock garden, while in Jukôin is the grave of the tea master Sen no Rikyû and National Treasure paintings by Shôei and Eitoku Kanô which date from the opening of Daitoku-ji.

Myôshin-ji Temple opened by the priest Musô has many important structures of the Momoyama and early Edo Periods. Included are the Sanmon Gate, Butsuden, Hattô, Bell Hall, Sutra Hall, Abbot's Chamber and the Bath (all ICA). Tan-yû Kanô executed the sliding door paintings in the Main Abbot's and the dragon on the ceiling inside the Sanmon Gate. Mishôan Pavilion and the Hiragara Gate (both ICA) are the oldest structures in the compound.

Teigyokuken Tea House
in Shinjuan

Subsidiary temples in Myôshin-ji dating from the Muromachi Period that should be visited are Reiun-in, with paintings (ICA) by Motonobu Kanô, and Taizô-in, with a rock garden said done by Motonobu and a National Treasure painting.

Garden by Motonobu Kano in Taizoin

The Kinkaku (Golden Pavilion) of Rokuon-ji Temple in Kitayama was reconstructed in 1955. Originally a mountain villa belonging to Yoshimitsu Ashikaga, it was turned into a Rinzai Sect temple after his death. Following along the simple fence by the Pavilion and climbing a set of stone steps, one comes to Sekkatei Pavilion. This tea house is a reconstruction of the late nineteenth century in the taste of Kanamori, an early seventeenth century priest.

◀ Kinkaku and pond of Rokuon-ji

Five-storied pagoda
of Ninna-ji

Tôji-in, a Rinzai Sect temple, preserves the grave of Takauji Ashikaga and wooden statues of the generations of the Ashikaga family. Seirentei Pavilion, in the garden behind the Abbot's Chamber, is a tea house in the combined shomin and buke style.

Ryôan-ji's rock garden is so famous that it requires but little comment. On white pebbles are placed fifteen stones in five groupings so aligned as to form a large arc. The original five stones date from the middle of the Muromachi Period (fifteenth century). By the beginning of the Edo Period the stones, added to over the years, came to number fifteen. Bamboo fences by the gardens to the east outside the Abbot's Chamber and to the west outside the Shoin are called the "Ryôan-ji-fence" and are particularly fitting for a Zen temple of the Rinzai Sect.

Ryôan-ji-fence

Kôryû-ji Temple in Uzumasa is best known for the wooden Miroku Bosatsu statue (NT) there, the oldest Buddhist statue in Kyoto. It was given to Kawakatsu Hata by Prince Shôtoku (574–622). Other statues in the National Treasure class from the Tempyô and Heian Periods make this a spot not to be overlooked. The Kamakura Period Main Hall (NT) of Keiguin in the same compound should also be seen.

Renge-ji Temple, just east of Ninna-ji, preserves stone bodhisattva of the early seventeenth century. A route rich in literary ties runs from Ninna-ji to Narabigaoka and Narutaki.

Miroku Bosatsu
in Kôryû-ji

Part of Kôryû-ji

Seirentei Pavilion and pond in Tôji-in

Stone Garden in Ryôan-ji

Katsumoto Hosokawa (1430–1473) came to possess Ryôan-ji when it was still a villa of the Tokudaiji family. It gradually grew as a Rinzai Sect temple. The stone garden evolved through the Zen instinct of generations of head priests.

Ninna-ji Temple of the Shingon Sect was founded in the ninth century. In addition to the celebrated Omuro cherry trees, the temple is known for its Kondô Hall (NT), Niômon Gate (ICA) and five-storied pagoda (ICA).

◀ Main Hall of Ninna-ji

Path to Kôzan-ji

Famous throughout Japan are the fresh verdure of spring and the blazing colors of autumn on Toga-no-o and Maki-no-o, where Kôzan-ji and Sai-myô-ji Temples are found, and Mt. Takao, where Jingo-ji Temple is located. All three places are near the Kiyotaki River. As a matter of fact, the entire Kiyotaki River area is known for cherry viewing and the colors of autumn. Many people also come here to hear the sounds of singing frog and little cuckoo.

Kôzan-ji is known for the Emaki of Chôjû Giga (picture scroll of bird and animal caricature) (NT) and for the Kamakura Period structure Sekisui-in (NT). Visitors here are impressed strongly with the view and the quiet of the beautiful walk. After looking at the Heian Period buddhas (NT) in Jingo-ji, the grave of Mongaku on the mountain behind the temple should be visited. From there Mt. Atago can be climbed.

◀ Latticed door in Sekisui-in of Kôzan-ji

On the way to the Kiyotaki River from Atago Shrine, Getsurin Temple is passed.

Saga was once mostly covered with large tracts of bamboo. Today, however, only Inner Saga and the land around Hirosawa Pond still permit viewing of the natural beauty for which the area had long been famous. One can still see old sections of Kyoto while traveling by bus to Takao from Narutaki in the eastern section of Sagano.

Ryôtoku-ji is a temple in the village of Narutaki. The incident is recalled here of the nun who offered St. Shinran a radish in winter and was rewarded with a cross written with pampas grass dipped in ink. Every year, on the ninth of December, believers gather here to partake of a special radish dish which they hope will help them in their emulation of the life of Shinran. The entire scene excludes a warmth that makes one forget the cold of the season.

Kiyotaki River ▶

Shooting Hozu Rapids

From March to August in 1606, twenty-five miles of river were cleared of rocks to open a water route. Today, the ten miles of the river from Kameoka City to Arashiyama is enjoyed as a thrilling boat ride, the Hozugawa Kudari.

In all the northern mountains there is not another view to match the view of the Kiyotaki River from Jingo-ji on Mt. Takao.

Looking down on Kiyotaki River from Takao ▶

42

KYOTO WEST

Hirosawa Pond was created by Kanjô, a grandson of the Emperor Uta, to be used for irrigating the surrounding area. The wooden statue, Fudô-myô-ô (ICA) of Henshô-ji, a temple once located here, is still preserved south of the pond. Northwest of the pond is found the mausoleum of the Emperor Gouta.

Along the northern shore of nearby Ôsawa Pond stand a group of Heian Period stone buddhas. Daikaku-ji, a monzeki temple of the Shingon Sect, is also near here, and allows viewing of glorious art form the Momoyama and early Edo Periods.

The statue of Shaka (NT) in Seiryô-ji was sent to Japan from Sung by the priest Chônen. This Saga type of Shaka has been copied in many parts of the country. Damaged by fire in 1218, the statue was later repaired by the famous sculptor Kaikei.

Hirosawa Pond   Stone buddhas near Ôsawa pond

Running east-west, the Ôi River divides Saga on the north from Arashiyama on the south. The entire stretch of mountains here was once called the Ogura Mountains, while Mt. Kameyama was the mountain directly in back of Tenryû-ji and Nison-in Temples. In the Kamakura Period, the Emperor Gosaga changed the names, so that Ogura referred to Mt. Kameyama alone.

Deities in Nison-in of Mt. Ogura are the Hokken Shaka and the Raigô Mida. Their statues are ICA of the Kamakura Period. Graves of the Nijô family, the Sanjô family, and Ryôi and Soan Suminokura are in the cemetery behind Mt. Ogura. The number of visitors to the cemetery has grown in recent years.

Main Hall of Seiryô-ji

Old stone grave markers in Nison-in

Mifune Festival on Ôi River

Centuries ago, when some of the first settlers came to Kyoto, part of the river was made into a sluice to allow boating for pleasure.

From the time when poetry competitions were held in autumn by the retired Emperor Uta, music has been a part of the recreation here. Kurumazaki Shrine, reviving the old tradition, holds the Mifune Boat Festival every year in early spring.

◀ Tenryû-ji pond created by Musô

47

Not far south from Nison-in is Jôjakkô-ji Temple of the Nichiren Sect. It was founded by Nittei with aid from Ryôi Suminokura met here with shipbuilders and captains from Wakegawa of Okayama Prefecture when he opened the course of Hozu River for domestic trade.

Below the slope to Nison-in are found Rakushisha hut — tied to the poet Bashô — and the grave of the Imperial Princess Uchiko, daughter of the Emperor Saga. The Princess was a famous poetess in the Chinese style of the Heian Period. It was in Rakushisha that the poet Kyorai Mukai prepared to meet Bashô. Kyorai and his disciples intended to serve the master persimmons, which grew in great number around the hut. In a single night, however, the ripened fruit of more than forty trees was blown down in high winds.

"Rakushisha" means "falling persimmon hut".

Nonomiya Shrine sits in a bamboo grove about halfway between Rakushisha and Tenryû-ji. Princess Tsuki-no-miya stayed here in preparation for her pilgrimage to the great Ise Shrine. Especially well-liked here are the brushwood fence and the simple black torii gate.

Rakushisha Hut

Tenryû-ji of the Rinzai Sect temple is located on the site of the former Kameyama Palace. The garden in Tenryû-ji, dating from the founding of the temple in the fourteenth century, borrows scenery from the mountains around it. Takauji Ashikaga founded the temple when the Emperor Godaigo was banished to Yoshino. The Emperor had passed time here as a child with his grand-

Black Torii gate of Nonomiya Shrine

father, the retired Emperor Kameyama. Yoshimitsu Ashikaga ranked this temple first among the five great Zen temples of Kyoto. Eight fires over the centuries have left only the garden to remind one of the original form.

Garden of Tenryû-ji

Shôkintei Pavilion of
Katsura Imperial Villa

Garden of Moss Temple

Construction of Katsura Imperial Villa was begun by Prince Toshihito Hachijô-no-miya, younger brother of the Emperor Goyôzei. Work was completed by the Prince's son Toshitada. The shoin group of buildings – Old Shoin, New Goten, and Middle Shoin – are lined on the northwestern shore of the garden pond. In the garden are seven pavilions, three islands, sixteen bridges, and twenty-three stone lanterns. Eight hand basing deepen the sense in the garden of devotion to tea.

The Zen garden of the Moss Temple, Saihô-ji, was constructed in 1339 by Soseki. Ôgon Pond in the lower garden is surrounded by moss. The middle garden, composed of rock and sand in the karesansui style, boasts of superlative stone groupings.

Hôrin-ji Temple of Arashiyama is dedicated to Kokû Bodhisattva. Boys and girls come here in pilgrimage when they reach thirteen years of age to pray for the gift of wisdom.

By following the slope along the river here you will come to Daihikaku, dedicated to Ryôi Suminokura.

The deity of Matsu-no-o Shrine, south from here on the west bank of the Katsura River, is Wake-ikazuchi, the god prayed to for the development of Yamashiro (Kyoto), Ômi and Tanba Provinces. It was from 701, under the auspices of the Hata Clan, that the shrine became really large. The Main Hall (ICA) seen today is a structure of the Muromachi Period. In the festival held by this shrine at the end of April, portable shrines are carried across the Katsura River.

Ume-no-miya Shrine is on the eastern bank of the Katsura River at Shijô Street. There is a beauty in its garden not seen elsewhere in Kyoto. Both Matsu-no-o and Ume-no-miya Shrines prospered with offerings from wealthy sake merchants. Ume-no-miya grew as the shrine of the Tachibana family.

Statue of Ryôi Suminokura in Daihikaku

52

The Moss Temple boasts of gardens constructed by Soseki. He effectively placed moss, pond, and stone groupings, harmonizing them even while getting the most out of their individual characteristics. In time, however, the garden around the pond and the space around the stone groupings of the middle garden came to be completely covered with moss. It is impossible today to appreciate the beauty of the rock garden, and the mountain and falls of the upper garden have practically disappeared. Holding religious significance, the falls should not be allowed to remain in its present state.

Enshrined in Ôharano Shrine on Mt. Nishiyama is the tutelary deity of the Fujiwara family of the early eighth century. In the same area is Shôji-ji Temple of the Tendai Sect famous for its cherry trees.

The road from Jûrin-ji Temple to Kômyô-ji Temple, where the mausoleum of St. Hônen is found, is most excellent for a walk in early spring or late fall.

Rock grouping in dry garden of Moss Temple

Yûzen dyeing is carried out largely in homes near the Horikawa River. Patterns are applied to the silk by hand, just as in the paste. Paste in the dye had been washed out of the fabric in waters of the Takano River, however you cannot find the beautiful scenery as below recently.

Washing yûzen fabrics

Main Hall of Kamo-mioya Shrine

Part of Shimo Goryô
Shrine Festival

The Lower Kamo Shrine is located near the junction of the Kamo and Takao Rivers. Its Main Hall (NT) lies secluded in Tadasu-no-mori.

The portable shrine carried in the festival of the shimo Goryô Shrine is elegantly beautiful.

View of Old Palace buildings from outside western wall

RAKUCHÛ: Central part of Kyoto

Central Kyoto in the Heian Period referred to the part of the capital outside the Palace Enclosure. Kyoto is of course larger today and, including the Old Imperial Palace grounds, is further east than when it was founded. Rakuchû, it follows, has also been widened. Area beyond what was formerly intended is included today.

In 1790, after ten months of work, and again in 1855, the Imperial Palace was restored to its Heian grandeur. In the Palace garden, one can recall the classics page by page in the solitude of this enclosure.

A little south and east of the Lower Kamo Shrine, at the Hyakumanben intersection, we found Kyoto University and Chion-ji, a temple with ties to St. Hônen. Coming west

Sakaimachi Gate of Old Palace   Main Hall of Shimo Goryô Shrine

again along Imadegawa Street, one finds Dôshisha University. Nearby are Ritsumeikan University and the Prefectural Medical College. A large part of the area just north and east of the old Palace is occupied by such institutions of learning.

Neighboring Dôshisha University is Shôkoku-ji Temple of the Rinzai Sect. Together with the Upper Goryô Shrine, Shôkoku-ji served as the headquarters for the army of Katsumoto Hosokawa during the Ônin Wars in the fifteenth century.

Lower Goryô Shrine, south of the Palace, guarded the Palace together with Upper Goryô Shrine. Since the eighth century the Lower Shrine gave spiritual protection to the capital from disease and misfortune. In it are enshrined the spirit of the Emperor Reigen. The front gate of the shrine is the former Kenrei Gate of the Imperial Palace.

Nijô Castle, on Horikawa Street, was a Detached Palace
from 1867 to 1939. Originally built by Ieyasu Tokugawa as
a mansion. Over the years, the tower and the inner castle
were destroyed by fire. Today, the garden of Ni-no-maru and
the Ni-no-maru Goten (NT) bring to mind the glory of the
past. Appreciation of the stone groupings in the garden is
fostered by the absence of the water.

Carriage entrance of Ni-no-maru Palace (NT) in Nijô Castle

Dolls recalling older days in Goten of Ni-no-maru

Doll statue in Hôkyô-ji

Kitano line streetcar

Main building of
Kitano Shrine

The first streetcar in Japan, the Kitano Line of Kyoto City, ran along the Horikawa River. It was only at the end of July in 1961 that the original narrow gauge cars were taken out of services. All along the river are the homes of dyers of Yûzen fabrics. The river was used to rinse the fabric, making the waterway a fantasy, at times.

The Textile Museum of the Nishijin area is on Imadegawa Street. At the time of the Ônin Wars, Nishijin was the site of the camp of the western army. The name "Nishijin", meaning "west camp" is a permanent reminder of what happened in history here. With the backing of Toyotomi Hideyoshi, the area became a textile area. In the middle of the Edo Period (eighteenth century) there were more than 5,000 weaving machines. Today, Nishijin products are sent to all parts of the country. It is even said that as Nishijin goes, so goes Kyoto.

Hôkyô-ji, a nunnery of the Zen sect, is located on Horikawa

Street north of Imadegawa Street in the Tera-no-uchi district, an area of many temples. An exhibition of Kyoto dolls is at Hôkyô-ji in spring and fall.

Northwest just a short way from the temple, along the small stream are found the homes of the tea families Ura and Omote Senke. These are two of the families which have perpetuated the traditional tea ceremony from the time of Sen no Rikyû.

Hôon-ji Temple is just northwest of the Senbon Imadegawa intersection. Its Main Hall (NT), dating from 1227, preserves an Inner Shrine and Alter in the Takamikura style. The Main Hall is in the best of the Shinden and Gyokuza styles. Enshrined here is a statue of Shaka (ICA) by Gyôkai which played an important role in developing understanding within the culture.

The Inner Shrine (NT) also has statues of ten disciples of Buddha by Kaikei and six statues by Jôkei. All sixteen statues are ICA. This is indeed a temple preserving the beauty of Kamakura Period architecture and sculpture.

Michizane Sugawara is enshrined west of Hôon-ji in Kitano Tenmangû Shrine. Hideyoshi ordered the construction of Kitano Shrine in his will. His son, Hideyori, commissioned one of his vassals to do the work. It was completed in 1607 in the classical gongen style.

If you return to the Modori Bridge on the Horikawa River and then walk south you will find the home of the potter Rakuke. Tea cups were made here for Hideyoshi. Centuries of experience have made Rakuke one of the most elegant pottery shops in Kyoto. Rakuyaki is the name of the style.

Oike Street

Oike Street runs east-west between Nijô and Sanjô Streets. The Gion Festival and Aoi Festival processions both pass here. The City Hall is on the corner of Oike and Kawara-machi Streets. Adding dignity to the same corner is a statue of Adam by Rodin.

Kamo River near Pontochô

Shijô-Kawaramachi is the busiest intersection in Kyoto.

The Kawaramachi Street runs along the Kamo River, and is one of the biggest shopping areas of Kyoto.

Pontochô is the quarter on the western bank of the Kamo River between Sanjô and Shijô Streets. Together with the Miyako Odori of the Gion Quarter, the Kamogawa Odori of Pontochô, held in spring and fall, deepens the seasonal feeling in Kyoto.

Shimabara, a former licensed quarter, had been located between Nishi and Higashi Hongan-ji Temples at Rokujô Misujimachi. It was moved in 1641 to the area south from Gojô and west from Ômiya Streets. In the Sumiya of Shimabara one can see what the most elegant geisha house of old looked like inside. The Wachigaiya, also in Shimabara, is another such remnant from days now past. The pillars inside Shimabara bear deep cuts left by samurai swords.

The tayû of Shimabara, women especially chosen for training in all the arts, are mistakenly classed with the oiran of Edo or the tenjin of Shimabara. Even today these women wear thirty kilograms of kimono and accessories. Only five remain today. All are here in Shimabara. In stricter days, the only women who could use vehicles or large umbrellas in the city were the wives and daughters of courtiers and tayû.

Sumiya of Shimabara

The Nijô Jin-ya (ICA) is south of Oike Street on Ômiya Street. It was the stopping place for daimyô who stayed in Kyoto but had no living quarters of their own city. Construction of this building took twenty years in the latter half of the seventeenth century. It holds the interest of all sight-seers, for its hiding places, into where the daimyô might run to protect his life from assasinators, and its fireproof structures were made skilfully in walls, ceilings, stairs, and other places. It is an excellent example of fine sukiya architectures.

Mibu Temple is north of Shimabara. Every year at the end of April the temple sponsors a program of amateur religious pantomime. It originated as offerings to Buddha for his help in combatting disease. This Mibu Kyôgen is most interesting for its ties to Kabuki drama.

Inside of Nijô Jin-ya

Religious pantomime at Mibu

Unfolding type of
Kyoto fans
(Kyô-uchiwa)

Folding type of
Kyoto fans
(Kyô-sensu)

Tayû of Shimabara preparing tea

Karamon Gate of Nishi Hongan-ji

Ishiyama Hongan-ji was a temple located on the land at
Osaka Castle. In 1592, Hideyoshi moved the temple to
Rokujô Street west of Horikawa in Kyoto. Ten years later,
in 1602, Ieyasu Tokugawa divided the temple in two. As
Nishi Hongan-ji and Higashi Hongan-ji, the two grew as great
temples of the Shinshû Sect. Kyô-nyo was made abbot of the
new Ôtani Hongan-ji located at the Karasuma Rokujô. His
younger brother Jun-nyo was made abbot of the other
Hongan-ji. Higashi (meaning east) Hongan-ji is Ôtani, and
Nishi (meaning west) Hongan-ji is Hongan-ji.

Nishi Hongan-ji suffered severe damage from a fire in
1617. From that time until about 1632 a number of structures were moved here from Fushimi Castle. One important
structure is the Daishoin (NT). The Karamon Gate (NT)
was originally from Fushimi Castle but did not come to
Nishi Hongan-ji directly. It came from the Hôkoku Mausoleum. Today, it stands before the entrance to the shoin.
The Hiunkaku Pavilion (NT) came from Jurakudai. The
Ôkakudai Bath (NT) was also moved here. The Mieidô was
completed in 1637.

Tragedy struck in 1788. The great Kyoto fire destroyed

Inside from Main
Gate of Higashi
Hongan-ji

not only Momoyama Period (sixteenth century) architecture but almost the entire Higashi Hongan-ji. From that time until the Meiji Restoration of 1868 the temple was rebuilt and leveled again by fire three times. The present Mieidô dates from 1895, while the large gate in front of the Mieidô was completed in 1911.

A Noh stage is found south of the large assembly hall and also in front of the White Shoin (NT) in Higashi Hongan-ji. The first is an ICA from Fushimi Castle. The second, the oldest Noh stage (NT) in existence, is said to be from Juraku-dai.

Outstanding paintings and sculptures are seen on the walls and ceilings of the White Shoin. Constantly changing color and design keep every corner alive with interest. It is here and in Nijô Castle that the art of the end of the sixteenth and the beginning of the seventeenth centuries can be enjoyed to your heart's content.

The Shinshû religion started with St. Shinran and grew in the Muromachi Period with the priest Ren-nyo. It has overcome myriad difficulties in its growth towards the magnitude of the Hongan-ji temples of today.

Fushimi Inari Shrine

Fushimi Inari Shrine is the headquarter of Inari Shrines which enshrine the gods of agriculture.

The five-storied pagoda (NT) of Tô-ji was built by Iemitsu Tokugawa in 1641, just four years after the pagoda at Ninna-ji. It is the largest pagoda in the city.

Five-storied pagoda (NT) of Tô-ji ▶

Nandaimon Gate and Kondô Hall of Tô-ji

Tô-ji (East Temple) was built in 796. Sai-ji (West Temple), now gone, was on the other side of Rashômon Gate. Fronting on Kujô Street, Tô-ji was originally four times the area what it is today. Its original measurements tell us much about how the old capital was laid out. In 823, Kûkai made this temple the home of the Shingon Sect, and two years later the Lecture Hall was completed. The Main Hall (NT) was built under Imperial command by Hideyori. North of the Main Hall, and dating from the same period, is another Lecture Hall (ICA).

The Nandaimon Gate (ICA) was moved here from Hôkô-ji Temple. All other gates here, including the especially superlative Renge Gate (NT), date from the Kamakura Period (twelfth to fourteenth centuries).

The Master's Hall (Daishidô) is a 1380 construction. It is in the old shinden style. The Kyakuden (NT), dating from 1606, is next to the North Gate (ICA). The Lecture Hall (ICA), preserving the fifteenth statues of Buddha since Kûkai founded the temple, was reconstructed with the Kondô (NT) in the Momoyama Period.

Rashômon Gate was erected west of Tô-ji at a distance

Rashômon Gate marker

the same as the east-west length of the temple. Skipping the same distance from Rashômon Gate again to the west, and utilizing the same area as for Tô-ji, Sai-ji Temple was constructed and Shubin became its first abbot. Only a marker today remains to show where Sai-ji once was.

North from Rashômon Gate, all the way to Nijô Street, was the more than eighty-meters wide Suzaku-Ôji. On the northern extreme of this road was the Suzaku Gate, the main gate to the Daidairi (the Great Palace Enclosure). Inside this enclosure were Chôdôin, with Ôtenmon as its gate, where important political ceremonies and festivities were held; Daigokuden, the central building; and Burakuin, set a little to the west, where ceremonies of state were carried out. The Dairi, or Inner Enclosure, was northwest of Chôdôin. It held the Imperial living quarters, the Shishin-den and Seiryô-den. Certain ceremonies and festivities connected to the Imperial Family were carried out in the Dairi. Later, when the Daigokuden disappeared, the events carried there were transfered to the Shishinden. The Dairi, the Imperial living quarters, thus came to serve also as the central organ of politics.

Garden of Sanbôin

Daigo-ji, a Shingon Sect Temple in the southern part of Yamashiro, is divided into Yamanoue (Upper) and Yamanoshita (Lower). It was founded in 907 by the priest Rigen. The five-storied pagoda (NT) still predominated since 951. From the period after 1598 when Hideyoshi came here for cherry viewing, his son of Hideyori worked on the restoration of Daigo-ji. It was through him that the Sanbôin garden, the Omote Shoin (NT), and other structures in the temple were completed.

◀ Five-storied pagoda of Daigo-ji

Gate in Sanbôin

DAIGO, UJI and SOUTH YAMASHIRO DISTRICTS

In the Upper Daigo-ji is a Prayer Hall (NT) dating from 1834. The Yakushi Hall (NT) was constructed in 1121 while the Yakushi statue (NT) is representative of the transitional style of the latter part of the ninth century.

The Kondô of the Lower Daigo-ji Temple is a Kamakura Period structure moved here from the Kishû area in 1600. Its Yakushi statue (ICA) is a beautiful example of sculpture from the same period.

Hideyoshi commissioned his gardener to work on the garden in Sanbôin. After his death (1598), however, it was completed.

The Inner Shoin (ICA) in Daigo-ji preserves a famous and fine set of shelves. A wonderful view presents itself from the Jôdan or raised room in the shoin. One famous stone was taken here from Jurakudai, Hideyoshi's mansion. Many daimyô presented other tremendous stones to the temple and they were placed left, right, front, and back to harmonize with the axis stone.

Chinese style
railing of
Manpuku-ji

At the foot of the mountain to the east of the Uji River near here is found Manpuku-ji Temple of the Ôbaku Sect. Opened in 1661, Manpuku-ji boasts of thirteen buildings and gates in the ICA class. Twenty-one consecutive generations of abbots here were from Ming and Ching of China. Examples of calligraphy by each of the abbots are preserved and may be viewed. Buddha images in Manpuku-ji are masterpieces by the naturalized Chinese sculptor Handôsei. So great is the chinese influence here that people who visit think they may have pilgrimaged to a Chinese temple.

Gate to right of Sanmon Gate

Sanmon Gate of Manpuku-ji

A villa in Uji belonging to Yorimichi Fujiwara was turned into the Byôdôin Temple in 1052 in memory of the two thousand years after the death of Buddha. The statue of the deity (NT) of the temple, Amida Nyorai, was done by Jôchô (d. 1057). Memorial bones of Michinaga, father of Yorinaga are preserved in the body of the Amida statue.

Eaves added to the Amida Hall (NT) of Byôdôin give it the appearance of being two-storied. Covered passageways to left and right from the hall, and turn into two other passageways leading to the Bôkaku (Tower).

Amida Hall of Byôdôin

Amida Statue of Byôdôin

Thirteen-storied pagoda (ICA) of Ukishima Island in Uji

The Uji Bridge, originally constructed in 646, is the oldest bridge in Japan illuminated for use by people and horses. There is a part of the bridge, between the second and third finial ornaments, that juts out a bit over the water.

Shien Eison of Saidai-ji Temple in Nara erected a thirteen-storied pagoda near here at thirteenth century, to appease the spirits of the fish in the river, and at that time he also reconstructed the bridge.

The Main Building (ICA) in Uji Shrine is a Muromachi Period structure. Also close to here, and not to be missed, is the Main Hall (NT) of the Upper Shrine.

Further upstream is Kôshô-ji Temple with its stone gate and Koto Slope. This temple, the most historical of the Sôtô Sect Zen temples, was opened by Dôgen (1200–1253).

Upper Uji Shrine

Stone gate of Kôshô-ji

San-no-ma of Uji Bridge, and Uji River

Iwashimizu Hachiman Shrine

The Yodo River flows along the southern edge of Kyoto. Located on Mt. Otokoyama near the river is Iwashimizu Hachiman Shrine, founded in 860.

The Main Building of Iwashimizu Shrine in the hachiman style was built in 1134. In the hachiman style, it is an ICA along with the gates of the other structures. There are sculptured works here dating from before 1624.

Sôjun Ikkyû, rivived Myôshô-ji and turned it into Shûon-an. In this temple there is the Butsuden (ICA) dating from the Muromachi Period. The garden south of the Abbot's Chamber is also from the Muromachi Period while the rock garden to the northeast was constructed by Keiando.

Grasshopper sculpture of Honden (ICA)

Garden of Shūon-an

Yodo River junction from Mt. Otokoyama

South on the street in front of Fushimi Inari Shrine is Fujinomori Shrine. In this shrine enshrined the gods protected the Yamashiro Province.

There are many mausoleum of the Emperors near here, for example the Momoyama Mausoleum of the Emperor and Empress Meiji. And also are there the statues of Gohyaku-Rakan in Sekihô-ji Temple, Tahôtô Pagoda (ICA) in Hôtô-ji Temple, and etc.

Not far from the Momoyama Mausoleum is Gokô-no-miya Shrine dedicated to the god Hachiman. Its front gate was originally the Omotemon Gate (ICA) of Fushimi Castle.

Across the Uji River on the far side of the Kangetsu Bridge are the remains of big Ôkura Pond, a spot made

almost into a lake long ago when waters from the river rushed in.

Hideyoshi built a levee on the left bank of the river here and the name given to the small body of water was Ogura Pond. Today, it has been turned into a rice paddy. Ogura, a tea production center, is part of Uji City.

Going south from here across the Kizu River, there are a stone marking the location of the first Imperial Palace in Yamashiro province, Shûon-ji Temple, and so on. Structures (ICA) and a rock garden made in about sixteenth century are there in Shûon-ji.

From here it might be well to visit Iwashimizu Hachiman Shrine and then to continue north along the west bank of the Kizu River.

Sosui Canal

The Canal into Kyoto from Lake Biwa, completed in 1890, required five years to construct. This canal provided Japan with its first water-generated electricity.

Panoramic night view of Modern Kyoto from Higashiyama

Takase River was opened by Ryôi Suminokura
and his son about 350 years ago.

Practicing Zen meditation in Ken-nin-ji

TRADITIONS OF KYOTO

Religious men, artisans in traditional industries, and others, persisted under unsatisfied wants, and fought continued hardships. Kyotoites in all walks of life struggled to keep Kyoto the main center of the country.

An example might be a weaver in the Nishijin area. An order for special tsuzure weave kimono might taken years to complete. During that period he might not even have money enough to pay for the living expenses of the members of his family. When he was paid from a daimyô for such an order, and he might not be paid, the amount could be less than the interest on borrowed money he had accumulated. Such artisans were all too numerous. The people who came to their aid were the traders of the city.

At the beginning of the seventeenth century, in order to revitalize Kyoto and especially Nishijin, special government plans were laid out. Nishijin was revived and Kyoto was

Tossing folding fans game of Hôkyô-ji

made into a large city.

It was the businessmen of that period who more than anyone else made the various festivals and events of Kyoto the gorgeous events they are today. The Gion Festival, the daimonji bonfire, and the fireworks at Mukaishima in Fushimi are examples of attraction in Kyoto.

On the other hands, various games which were one of the nobility since ninth century are handed down by Kyoto-ites. For example, the tossing holding fans game of Hôkyô-ji Temple is one of such games.

Priests, businessmen, and scholars all came to possess the spirit of Kyoto. When together they hurled themselves at the bakufu government, the glory of Kyoto became even more evident. Kyoto, the capital and site of the Imperial Palace, and also the center of art and learning was indeed a unique city.

Noh play by firelight at Heian Shrine in early June

Kyoto was also a center for spread of the arts. The first page in the history of Noh plays was written in Kyoto at fourteenth century.

The three Senke families and the Yabunouchi family, all of Kyoto, are the chief schools of tea in Japan today. Traditional flower arrangement is transmitted by the Ikenobô School. Other flower schools in Kyoto boasting of tradition are schools of Daikaku, Ninna-ji, and Senkei.

Open-air tea ceremony of Kitano Tenmangû Shrine ▶

There are many kinds of traditionally industrial arts in Kyoto, for example the pottery and china of Kiyomizu-yaki, the textile of Nishijin-ori, etc. These are suitable souvenir of Kyoto for both Japanese and foreigners who come to Kyoto.

Kiyomizuyaki is the most popular in Kyoto. It holds a tradition of ratistic pottery, and is continued to produce at near Kiyomizu Temple. It is said that Kiyomizuyaki was already produced in early of the seventeenth century. About the middle of that century it was begun to produce the colorful-painting ceramics, to be said Koshimizu, and the

Making scene of Kiyomizuyaki

quantity of these production was increased. Since the end of eighteenth century, the china has got the position of main production of Kiyomizuyaki instead of pottery. Now many dinner sets are produced here to be exported to many countries.

Nishijin-ori which is famous in the world still continues to weave at Nishijin of Kyoto since the end of sixteenth century. It uses the silk as the raw material and is known as one of the highest grade textile in Japan. Not only the kimono and obi but also the necktie, dress, gown, table cloth, and others are made of the Nishijin-ori.

Weaving factory of Nishijin-ori

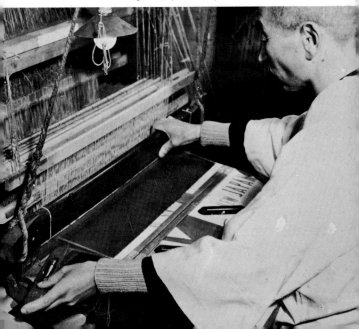

Miyako Odori

◀ Geisha from Pontochô

Kamogawa Odori

95

Kyoto Station

Kyoto South Interchange of Meishin Expressway

HISTORY OF KYOTO

Kyoto Station on the Municipal Subway No.1 Line
(see p.124 for details)

ANCIENT KYOTO

Kyoto before 794

Kyoto is located in a wide basin enclosed on three sides by mountains. The land to the south slopes gently until it eventually reaches the sea. The Kamo River flows down the east side of the basin from the north. The Katsura River outlines another land division as it flows down the west side of the basin. Further south the Kamo River cuts over from the east to join the Katsura River. In ancient times, this basin was known as Yamashiro. The center of urban development in Yamashiro was the Uda area.

Naturalized foreign tribes originally settled in Yamashiro. By the second half of the sixth century seven thousand families lived in the Katsura River basin. Collectively, they were known as Hata families. They brought prosperity to the Matsu-no-o Shrine, the Inari Shrine and Kôryû-ji Temple in western Kyoto. A second large settlement, located on the Kamo River side of the basin, divided Yamashiro.

The Yamashiro clans and naturalized foreign tribes contributed to the area's development. By the eighth century, Kyoto (Uda) was a quite prosperous urban center. Together with prosperity, struggles for power ensued. Rivalry between aristocratic groups was accelerated by shifting alliances with the monks of powerful Nara Buddhism.

Heian Kyô and Heian Buddhism

In 795, Emperor Kammu designated Uda "Heian Kyô," the Capital of Peace. The Daidairi Ceremonial Hall was completed in 795, and shortly thereafter the residents of the Nagaoka

Capital transferred to Sakyô, east of the central Suzaku-Ôji Road, and to Ukyô, west of the same road. In the fall of 795, an Imperial proclamation was issued to establish the Heian Capital. The great enterprises which made the move possible in turn owed their strength largely to the financial power and efforts of the people who settled in Yamashiro.

In 796, the Tô-ji and Sai-ji Temples were built, respectively, east and west of Rashômon Gate, the main gate to the Capital. Just before he died, Emperor Kammu granted permission to Saichô to establish the Enryaku-ji Temple to undertake the study of Tendai Hokkeshû Buddhism. The Emperor could not have imagined the historical role Enryaku-ji would play in Kyoto's history.

Influenced by esoteric Buddhism, the Tendai and Shingon sects contributed greatly to cultural developments in the Heian period. The fine Kônin and Jôgan art modes of the early ninth century derive from Buddhist influences.

Emperors Saga and Junna and Empress Danrin concerned themselves with the public welfare and initiated various civic improvements. Especially noteworthy was their interest in creating general academic improvements. Under their prodding, numerous constructions and repairs were affected in the western part of the Capital. The Emperor Ninmyô, meanwhile, was instrumental in raising the general level of Japanese art consciousness, particularly regarding foreign music.

Fujiwara Despotism

The Fujiwara family ascended to a powerful political position through a series of skillful marriage arrangements. The times permitted aristocrats to live lavishly, and the Fujiwaras set the example that everyone emulated. The Kasuga Shrine in Nara symbolized the family's strength while serving as its religious protector.

Various quarters prayed for heavenly intervention to check the despotism of the Fujiwaras. It seemed that a patron god was needed, that only a shrine more famous than Kasuga could strike them down. The Hachiman deity eventually assumed this role, and considerable efforts were extended to give Hachiman shrines prime national importance.

Imperially Descended Monks

Kûya was a monk of Imperial lineage who turned his eyes and heart toward the common people. He truly expressed the "merciful mind," and journeyed throughout Japan administering to the sick and burying the dead. He also founded Saikô-ji Temple, known today as Rokuharamitsu-ji. The temple retains its original Buddhist images.

The work of monks like Kûya increased Tadahira Fujiwara's prestige and lengthened his rule. The monks also brought honor and esteem to successive emperors, and propagated Heian Buddhism.

The rules of Tadahira and Morosuke Fujiwara led to increased trust of the Fujiwara family from both inside and outside the Court. The Imperial Palace was no longer the only place of wealth. The residences of the Sesshô and the Kampaku families became equally splendid. This was the dawn of Michinaga's rule, and was near the end of a two thousand year period following Shaka's death. In Buddhism, the first five hundred years after Buddha's death are called Gedatsukengô, while the second five hundred are called Zenjôkengô. Together, the first one thousand years are called the Shôhô, and during this period Shaka's teachings were believed in with complete and unfailing devotion. The third five hundred years are called Tamonkengô, and the fourth, Zôtôkengô. The second thousand-year period is called the Zôhô. While the influence of Buddha's teachings remained great during the Zôhô, Buddhists believed that sincere devotion in building many pagodas and temples was the way to ensure eternal salvation for themselves and their ancestors. Buddhism was brought to Japan in the last year of Tamonkengô.

In the last year of Zôtôkengô (1052), Michinaga's son Yorimichi converted his villa into a temple and named it Byôdôin. The temple became Michinaga's final resting place, and his bones were placed inside the statue of Jôroku Amida.

Midô worship was widespread about this time. A Midô is a small chapel-like shrine which houses an Amida Nyorai image. Efforts to create a heavenly paradise on earth excited developments in architecture, painting, sculpture and other arts and crafts. Literature also witnessed great advances. Jôchô, Murasaki Shikibu and Seishônagon were active during this period. Although the culture and arts retain the Fujiwara elegance, some aspects – such as Unkei's sculpture – reveal a strong masculine quality.

Sanjûsangendô

Kiyomori Taira constantly threatened the Emperor Goshirakawa's position. When the Emperor decreed that 1001 Kannon statues be produced to win Kiyomori's collaboration, he proved his superior influence. The 1001 Kannon statues are enshrined in the Sanjûsangendô Temple, a great undertaking by the Emperor Goshirakawa to create political stability and bring religious assurances to a troubled populace.

Goshirakawa paid particular attention to the welfare of his subjects. He had idiosyncrasies too, like encouraging development of Imayô-uta, a form of popular singing.

MEDIEVAL KYOTO

Religious and Political Change

The end of the twelfth century was a stormy age in Japan, charged with energy and potential. It was a time of action and change. Friction between ambitious lords was incessant, and religious innovations spread across the land.

The power struggle between the Genji and Taira clans accelerated the growth of the provincial warrior chiefs, who were destined to assume political leadership. Minamoto Yoritomo completely defeated the Taira clan in 1185. In 1192, he inaugurated the Kamakura "curtain" government.

About this same time, Hônen began preaching for a new sect that aimed at revigorating the spirit and initiative of the population. He helped to put new life into religious groups to combat political and secular suppression.

Ideas sifted from many Buddhist sects found fervent expression during this period. Monks made frequent pilgrimmages to China, considered the true source of Buddhist thought. The Jôdô (Pure Land) and Zen sects contributed to medieval Kyoto's culture much as Tendai and Shingon sects did in the Heian period. The influences of China's Sung and Yüan cultures, carried to Japan by Zen monks, were particularly effective in altering traditions of Heian culture.

Yoritomo reconstructed To-ji and Jingo-ji Temples, and his son Yoriie established Kennin-ji Temple. They intended to perpetuate the traditions of Heian Buddhism and contribute to Zen's prosperity. Zen Buddhism truly expressed the warrior spirit, and a general influence from the warrior class prevailed over Kyoto culture during this period. Also, after three generations of the Minamoto family, political power shifted in the Kamakura period to the Hôjô family.

Buddhist tenets became varied and complex. Shunjô established Sennyû-ji Temple and opened a Buddhist school there. Zen, Jôdô, Shingon and Tendai Buddhism all were studied. The relation between the Imperial Family and Sennyû-ji dates from this time.

Sanjûsangendô was destroyed in the great fire of 1248. The Sesshô (Regent) Kujô Michiie reconstructed that temple and built Tôfuku-ji Temple. Michiie died before the two structures were completed and the work was carried on by his son. Only thirteen per cent of the 1001 Kannon statues in Sanjûsangendô escaped damage in the fire. The others were restored by Tankei, son of Unkei. They were the finest works of his later years.

Tankei's sculptures are said to possess a curious hypnotic power. Should a believer recognize the face of someone deceased in one of the Kannon faces, he will experience this strange sensation.

The Mongol Invasions

In 1281 the second and largest of two Mongol invasions spread anxiety across the country. Preparations were made to meet the oncoming hordes. The nobles, the warriors and the common people all prayed for heavenly intercession. As the invaders were crossing the sea a great storm struck and devasted their ships. The few Mongols who reached the shore of Japan were defeated easily. In their ignorance the people accepted the storm as a display of divine power. The storm came to be known as the Kamikaze, "divine wind."

Japan's rulers had made excellent military preparations for

the Mongol invasion, and their spirits were buoyant after the victory. The Hôjôs in Kamakura seemed from that point to pursue a life of total pleasure at the expense of the public good.

Emperor Kameyama and Nanzen-ji Temple

Even Emperor Kameyama was not free from over-indulgences. After Dôchi's death, his Eikandô residence in Zenrin-ji Temple was turned into a villa by the Emperor. This extreme luxury shocked Kyotoites. A rumor persisted that because of rumblings amongst the people, ghosts were stalking the Palace. The rumor worried the Emperor and he persuaded Mukanfumon, a monk of Tôfuku-ji Temple, to conduct a service to satisfy the spirits. He converted the villa into a Zen temple and named it Nanzen-ji. This incident suggests that the people deeply distrusted the Emperor.

Hôjô's Decline and Emperor Godaigo

Following the Mongolian defeat, discord and disorder ran rife in the Hôjô curtain government. Keenly aware of a golden opportunity to overthrow the Hôjô, the Emperor Godaigo set about organizing his forces. His plan was exposed, however, and the Hôjô exiled him to Oki Island in the Japan Sea. The year was 1332. A move for his return was immediately set in motion by loyalists.

The Godaigo incident prompted the Hôjô to strengthen its position. The family set up a second Emperor to fake imperial cooperation. Their choice was Kôgon-in, a prince of Gofushimi Jôkô. His mother's residence, incidentally, called the Dairi, developed into the present Kyoto Palace.

Godaigo had many loyal followers, and his most able

generals persisted in their military ventures against the Hôjô. Ashikaga fought at Rokuhara, while Nitta Yoshisada attacked Kamakura. They finally were victorious and returned Godaigo after only a year in exile.

Godaigo had become a devout Zen Buddhist. He named Musô Kokushi as the chief priest of Nanzen-ji, and in 1334 added that temple to the list of Five Great Zen Temples.

The Rise of Ashikaga

The Hôjô curtain government's defeat marked the Kenmu Restoration, yet there were still powerful Hôjô forces in Kamakura. Original strategy called for Yoshisada to rout the remaining Hôjô troops. At any rate, Yoshisada would lose face if Takauji went instead to engage the enemy. He worked behind the scenes to persuade the Emperor not to send Takauji. Takauji, however, proceeded on his own to Kamakura. He evidently feared losing the whole campaign by leaving some Hôjô armies intact. Against Takauji's superior might the Hôjô forces collapsed in total defeat. Takauji won the military victory, but Yoshisada strongly suggested that he had betrayed the Emperor in so doing. His ignominious position is understandable. He was from an eminent Genji family and would have gained much real influence if he could have established a Genji government. As it developed, Takauji was called an enemy of the Imperial Court.

This period, the Nanbokuchô, witnessed unusual political strife and fierce wars. It began with the return of Godaigo from exile and continued for a period of fifty-eight years. The Kamakura curtain government collapsed and a new one was established in Kyoto with support from new feudal lords called

Daimyô. Besides the struggles between new and old warrior groups, there was another political faction which aimed to renew the Heian governing system. Nanbokuchô ended with the legitimates succession to the throne of Emperor Gokameyama of Nanchô, who adopted Gokomatsuin of Hokuchô. Real political power was in the hands of Ashikaga Yoshimitsu's Muromachi bakufu government.

Mainly because the Ashikaga family and Yoshisada were bitter rivals the Kenmu Restoration did not develop into a united effort. Ashikaga grew more powerful and eventually marshalled forces in a revolt against Emperor Godaigo. The Emperor was forced to flee to Yoshino near Nara. Ashikaga occupied Kyoto and in addition to establishing his own government he named another Emperor to the throne. Japan thus came to have two emperors, and their respective residences are referred to as the Northern and Southern Courts (Nanbokuchô). One result of Ashikaga overthrowing the Imperial Court was a fusion of Heian and Kamakura cultures.

Zen in the Nanbokuchô Period

After Godaigo died in 1339, Saihô-ji Temple in Kyoto was renamed Saihôzen-ji. Hônen and Shinran Buddhism had flourished in Saihô-ji, and numerous pagodas were built and interconnected with special walks. Gorgeous stone gardens were built in wonderful harmony with a pond and a great variety of mosses. Waterfalls were arranged so that the water cascaded over three strata of rocks. The landscape was an artistic composition utilizing water, stone, sand and moss. The elements combined to create majestic scale and a delicate sense of texture. Today, this same temple is known as Kokedera, the

Moss Temple.

Kenminsen (Trading Ships) and Muromachi Culture

While Tenryû-ji Temple in Kyoto was still under construction funds ran out. Usually, money for temple constructions was raised through taxes. The populace had been seriously overtaxed from continuous wars, however, and the priest Soseki considered other possibilities to raise money. He appealed to the government to initiate trade with China. The Ashikaga did open trade, and it proved highly profitable. Tenryû-ji was completed with revenue gained from the trade. The success and frequency of trade arrangements, incidentally, resulted in Chinese money being used in Japan.

The Muromachi period also witnessed considerable artistic activity. Some famous artists were Kan-ami, Zeami, Zenchiku, Soami, Shingyô, Sôgi, Sesshû, Shukô and Ikenobô. It was also during this time that the Yamaboko floats of the Gion Festival assumed the form we see today.

The Ônin Wars began in 1467 and raged for ten years between the Hosokawa group on the west and the Yamana group on the east. Kyoto and its suburbs were devastated. It was after the Ônin Wars that Yoshimasa, pursuing a life of luxury, built Ginkaku-ji Temple, the Silver Pavilion.

The people themselves rose in protest against the government even prior to the Ônin Wars. Exploitation was widespread under the Ashikaga, and riots occured frequently, although leaders knew they would be punished with death.

Nishijin: the Weaving Center

The weavers of Kyoto had a tradition which traced back

to the Heian period. They left Kyoto during the Ônin Wars, but returned afterwards to settle in Shirakumo and Nishijin. The latter area gradually became the center of Japan's weaving industry.

In 1543, a Portuese ship visited Tanegashima Island off southern Kyushu and instigated rich trading in raw silk. Later, the merchant vessels, both Chinese and Portuese, began putting in at Nagasaki. Merchants of Sakai, near Osaka and Kyoto, travelled to Nagasaki to buy the silk. The import of raw silk aided Nishijin to develop, and by 1568 the area was prospering.

During long, bitter civil wars, Nishijin merchants played an important role for ensuring Kyoto's recovery. Rennyô's construction of Hongan-ji Temple also lifted the spirits of Kyotoites. Ikkyû Sôjun, one of Emperor Gokomatsu's children, rebuilt Daitoku-ji with financial support from Sakai merchants. His undertaking served as an example to the militarists, and greatly pleased the citizens.

Zen Gardens

Painting and literature by Zen monks also developed during this time. Monks designed karesansui (dry gardens) to represent the black and white landscape paintings of China. The gardens were simple productions built usually near a veranda and using stone, sand and a few plants. Zen gardens differed greatly from Soseki gardens. Eventually, Zen's austerity was distilled and represented with an arrangement of fifteen stones. This style can be viewed in Daisen-in and Shinjuan. Sekitei of Ryôan-ji Temple, the most famous Zen garden, has a special group of stones for viewing from a veranda.

It is a tranquil garden suggesting a Karesansui. In Tôfuku-ji Temple, Fundain used crane and turtle images to create a Hôraijima garden. The aim is to provide a landing place for Buddha. Rakans (servants) are set as though trying to reach Buddha to receive his teachings. Other stones are arranged to suggest Rakans who are turning away, having decided not to listen to Buddha. Sesshû supposedly originated the latter arrangement.

KYOTO'S MODERN HISTORY

Communication between Japan and the west began in the middle of the sixteenth century. It is perhaps best to call the beginning a "contact," since Japanese ships did not in turn visit the west. A parallel to the national unification that Nobunaga affected is the foreign trade developed by Hideyoshi and Ieyasu, although trade was severely checked in the early seventeenth century. The years that Nobunaga and Hideyoshi ruled were rich not only in terms of trade but also in art. Developments in the tea ceremony, painting and architecture were notable. This, the Azuchi-Momoyama period, is called the Japanese Renaissance.

In 1550, when Francis Xavier visited Kyoto, both the Court and the curtain government were exhausted by civil wars, and the Jesuit did not complete his mission. The Saint died enroute home from Japan. As an expression of their sadness some Kyoto people built a modest Nanban-ji Temple for him in 1568. A Nanban-ji is a special place of worship for foreign religions. In later years, a superstition grew that the good fortune brought in the form of raw silk in Portugese, Dutch and Chinese ships was tied to this Nanban-ji.

Nishijin came to produce fabrics and garments as fine as those of China and the west. The merchants and weavers had grown prosperous from foreign trade and entreated Hideyoshi to expand the trade. While agreeing to expand trade ties, he simultaneously launched an invasion of the Korean peninsula in 1592. He died in 1598, and the invasion troops returned to Japan. Without his leadership many policies and plans he designed were shelved. In 1604, however, Ieyasu strengthened

foreign relations and trade. By 1633, the quantity of trade
had multiplied many times. Besides importing raw silk, more-
over, Nishijin silk was being exported. A great amount of
wealth was accumulated in Japan, and rich merchant families
emerged.

During the Momoyama period Nishijin material became
prized among daimyô and wealthy provincial families. Weaving
techniques were gradually improved, and the merchants continued Kyoto's entire economy. As Nishijin went, so went
Kyoto.

Of course, industry expanded in other directions simultaneously to meet ever-widening domestic demands. The tea
ceremony, for example, excited developments in pottery and
in various industries that produced tea utensils. Gorgeous
decorations marked Momoyama architecture, and marvelous
sculptures filled the temples. The Sanjô Bridge was completed
in the late sixteenth century, and river banks called odoi were
constructed about the city. The Great Buddha of Hôkô-ji
Temple was finished in 1600.

Japanese Renaissance

Chronologically, the Keichô (1596–1614), Genna
(1615–23) and Kan-ei (1624–43) eras mark the early Edo
Period; in terms of architecture, gardening and the fine arts,
however, they cannot be clearly separated from the Azuchi-
Momoyama period. Fine scholars and artists active in these
years produced works that deeply influenced later generations.
Sôan Sumikura and Kôetsu Hon-ami wrote renowned language
texts and chants for Noh drama. Emperor Goyôzei published
several books on Japanese history. Yoshida Kyûan used

illustrations in a book on mathematic principles, the Jingoki. His explanations were clear enough for young and old alike to understand. The Jingoki was the best-selling book in the Edo Period, which perhaps indicates the high intellectual demand of the time. This era was truly a Japanese Renaissance.

Movement for Restoring the Imperial Court

During the early Edo Period the bakufu exerted great pressure on the Court and controlled the Emperor. Emperor Reigen (reigned 1663–87), with cooperation from loyalist supporters, resisted bakufu pressure and attempted to regain authority. He gained support from Ansai Yamazaki's Shintô teachings, which asserted the Emperor's divine lineage. Ansai preached at the Shimogoryô, Inari and Kamo Shrines. He also introduced Suika Shintoism teachings which infused natural history and Confucianism into Shintô doctrine. His undertakings, blessed with Emperor Reigen's complete approval, marks the beginning of the Tôbaku movement. Suika Shintoism was influential to the last days of the shogunate. Tokugawa Mitsukuni, meanwhile, initiated a project to edit an Imperial Court History (Dainihonshi), and his efforts were continued by the Yamazaki school. The endeavor greatly contributed toward reestablishing the Court.

The Ups and Downs of Nishijin

Urban Kyoto continued to expand. In 1681 it boasted more than 47,000 families and a population of 577,548. Nishijin weaving was the central factor in Kyoto's prosperity. Production in Nishijin increased markedly in the second half of the seventeenth century, and by 1703 the area had grown to include more than 5,000 houses and 10,000 weaving machines. Some weaving houses opened branches in Edo and Osaka.

Following the Genroku Period (1688–1703), Nishijin suffered a decline in its fortunes, partly due to competition from weaving centers that developed in other districts and partly to devastating fires in 1730 and 1788. Recovery was slow, but 2,000 weaving houses were in operation during the early nineteenth century.

The so-called Tempô Reforms of 1841, however, introduced to conserve funds and combat famine which spread in the wake of fires and riots, prohibited a long list of Luxuries, from publishing to prostitution. Nishijin weaving was included in the prohibition, and the cessation of all weaving activity turned the Nishijin area into a death-town.

The Great Merchant Families

The rise of the great merchant family of Mitsui Echigoya dates from the latter half of the seventeenth century. Main store stood at the corner of Nijô and Horikawa streets in Kyoto. Nishijin silk was sold for cash, and reasonable prices attracted many customers. Their branch store in Edo (Tokyo) was also successful. Daimaru, a competitor, opened a store in Fushimi, and in the early eighteenth century established stores at Imadegawa and Ômiya streets and in Matsubara. Branch stores were located in Edo, Osaka and Nagoya. Today, Daimaru and Mitsukoshi (formerly Mitsui Echigoya) are among the largest department stores in Japan and maintain branches in Tokyo, Osaka and Kyoto and many other cities.

Kyoto's financial center developed east of Koromo-no-tana and Muromachi streets, an area known for its numerous kimono material shops. Moneylenders prospered in Kyoto throughout the latter half of the seventeenth century. They lent to daimyô at high interest vates, but not infrequently went bankrupt when the money owed them was not repaid.

After the Genroku Period the bakufu depended on Kyoto money to support its banking system. Bank notes (kawase) came into use to permit ready transfer of money between Edo, Osaka and Kyoto.

The center of politics, meanwhile, shifted from Kyoto products, particularly rice. Kyoto boasted the highest financial prosperity during the Edo Period, largely due to its silk thread and materials industries and to financing.

Special Arts and Industries

The industrial art of Kyoto dyeing (kyôzome) developed along the banks of the Kamo and Hori rivers. That of Kyoto pottery (kyôyaki) grew at Kitayama and Higashiyama. Yûzen, a famous designer of materials and art crafts, contributed also to the art of dyeing fabrics.

The course of pottery development was inseparably linked with prevailing fashions in the tea ceremony. During the Edo period the design of tea houses was pursued with artistic zeal. Prince Tomotada built Katsura Imperial Villa; Emperor Gomizuno-o completed Shugakuin Imperial Villa. Such villas represented a full adaptation of tea ceremony taste on an imcomparable scale.

The Kanze, Hôshô, Kongô and Ôe schools flourished in

the Noh theater. Prosperity kept specialists in masks, costumes and Noh stages busily occupied. Fabulous decorative paintings were painted as backdrops for the plays. Ogata Kôrin drew natural scenes while Ike-no-taiga focused on paintings of people (bunjinga). Matsumura Keibun consolidated the various Kyoto schools of painting when he founded the Shijô school.

Kuruwa

The center of entertainment and the influence of its various establishments shifted occasionally in the early years of Kyoto. In the middle seventeenth century, however, Shimabara emerged as the hub of the pleasure world and exercised effective control over all pleasure areas (kuruwa) in the city. Exclusive to Shimabara were the tayû, young women of chastity, culture and artistic training. They were permitted to enter the court and were symbols of courtly prestige. The costume of tayû was distinguished by its special long-sleeved kimono, called uchikake. The attention paid the gorgeously dressed tayû helped bring prosperity to Nishijin weaving and to Kyôzome dyeing.

The Gion Quarter expanded during the prosperous Genroku Period (1689–1703). Its role as the setting for the wellknown play Chûshingura further spread its fame and popularity.

In and around Gion several types of female entertainers became popular. The first of these were the furisode, young girls who wore a special long-sleeved kimono. They were the only young girls out at night and were dressed in bright-colored kimono. They naturally attracted the attention of samurai and government officers. The young girls introduced these men to the older geisha. Furisode are the forerunners of today's maiko.

Hikiko were girls particularly adept at playing the samisen, and were also called geiko or geisha. After an apprenticeship-like tenure, maiko became geiko. Such titles, progressively more prestigious, culminated with the oiran, a colorfully-decorated, high-class prostitute who was distinct from and underwent quite different training from the geiko.

These entertainers performed a style of dance called kyômai. It developed from the Inoue school of dancing. The founder had served in the court and adapted various aristocratic manners to the dance. Gestures from Noh and Bunraku (puppet theater) were also added.

Folk Arts

Mibu Kyôgen, a religious pantomime, originated in the early fourteenth century at Mibu Temple in central Kyoto and is still performed there in Mibu Kyôgen, divine power defeats and expulses illness and disaster. Mibu Kyôgen was popularized by adding to it folk tales and elements from Noh. The play Tsuchigumo is directly adapted from Noh.

Rokusai nenbutsu is a religious dance to comfort the souls of the dead. Kûya (903–972) may have originated Rokusai Nenbutsu for his disciples as six days of singing and dancing meant to be mental preparation for memorial services to their ancestors. Another theory calls it a memorial service for the fallen soldiers of Akechi Mitsuhide's army, defeated by Hideyoshi. It is a lively dance performed to the accompaniment of bells and drums.

Old Imperial Palace

The Beginning of the Education System

Japan's formal school system dates from 1868, the first year of the Meiji era. Kyoto's Ryûchi Shôgakkô was the first primary school in Japan. By 1870, sixty-four primary schools had been built. The first high school, now known as Rakuhoku High School, was established at Kyoto Shoshidai-ato in 1871. In 1872 the first women's school opened. Today it is called Ôki High School.

Inauguration of the Emperor

The most important ceremony in an Emperor's reign is his inauguration ceremony, the Sokui-no-tairei. It is a grand occasion on which his accession to the throne is proclaimed to the world. Sokui-no-tairei continued to be held in Kyoto through the Taishô and Shôwa eras even though the capital had been moved to Edo in 1868, an attestation to the pervading dignity of Kyoto.

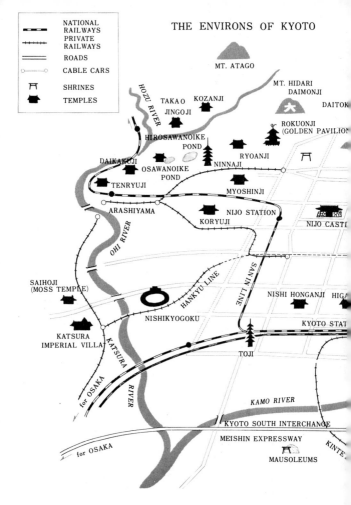

THE ENVIRONS OF KYOTO

NATIONAL RAILWAYS
PRIVATE RAILWAYS
ROADS
CABLE CARS
SHRINES
TEMPLES

MT. ATAGO

MT. HIDARI DAIMONJI

DAITOK

HOZU RIVER

TAKAO   KOZANJI
JINGOJI

ROKUONJI
(GOLDEN PAVILION

HIROSAWANOIKE POND

DAIKAKUJI   RYOANJI

OSAWANOIKE POND   NINNAJI

TENRYUJI   MYOSHINJI

OHI RIVER

ARASHIYAMA   NIJO STATION

KORYUJI   NIJO CASTLE

SAIHOJI
(MOSS TEMPLE)   HANKYU LINE

NISHI HONGANJI   HIGA

SAN IN LINE

NISHIKYOGOKU   KYOTO STAT

KATSURA
IMPERIAL VILLA   TOJI

for OSAKA

KATSURA RIVER

KAMO RIVER

KYOTO SOUTH INTERCHANGE

for OSAKA   MEISHIN EXPRESSWAY   KINTE

MAUSOLEUMS

120

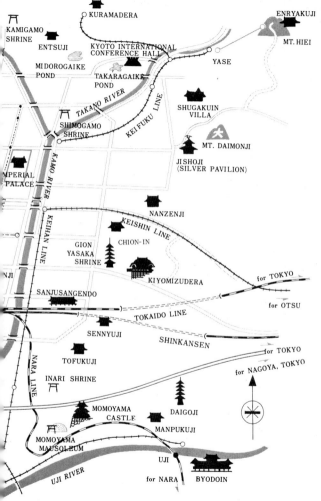

KURAMADERA

ENRYAKUJI

KAMIGAMO
SHRINE

MT. HIEI

ENTSUJI

KYOTO INTERNATIONAL
CONFERENCE HALL

MIDOROGAIKE
POND

YASE

TAKARAGAIKE
POND

TAKANO RIVER

KEIFUKU LINE

SHIMOGAMO
SHRINE

SHUGAKUIN
VILLA

MT. DAIMONJI

JISHOJI
(SILVER PAVILION)

IMPERIAL
PALACE

NANZENJI

KEISHIN LINE

GION
YASAKA
SHRINE

CHION-IN

KIYOMIZUDERA

for TOKYO

SANJUSANGENDO

for OTSU

TOKAIDO LINE

SENNYUJI

SHINKANSEN

TOFUKUJI

for TOKYO

INARI SHRINE

for NAGOYA, TOKYO

DAIGOJI

MOMOYAMA
CASTLE

MANPUKUJI

MOMOYAMA
MAUSOLEUM

UJI

UJI RIVER

for NARA

BYODOIN

MAIN ANNUAL EVENTS

MIYAKO ODORI (Apr. 1 – May 18 or thereabouts)
Miyako Odori is a colorful dance event staged by geisha of the Gion Quarter at the Kaburenjô Hall in Gion.

KAMOGAWA ODORI (Apr. 15 – May 20 or thereabouts)
Kamogawa Odori is a dance event staged by geisha of the Pontochô Quarter at the Kaburenjô Hall in Pontochô.

MIBU KYÔGEN (Apr. 21–29)
This Kyôgen, religious pantomime, is held with an annual religious service at the Mibu Temple every day during this period. Kyôgen plays are performed by amateurs from the parish. Actors wear wooden masks and the plays are accompanied by music from bells, flutes and drums.

AOI FESTIVAL (May 15)
The Aoi Festival is one of the three largest festivals in Kyoto, and one of the most colorful festivals in Japan.

MIFUNE FESTIVAL (3rd Sunday of May)
In this festival the atmosphere of the Heian Period (794–1185) is reproduced at Arashiyama Park. Called the Boat Festival, it is produced by Kurumazaki Shrine of Saga.

TAKIGI NOH (June 1, 2)
On the nights of June 1st and 2nd, Noh plays are performed on an outdoor stage and lighted by bonfires and

bare electric lights. This event takes place in the Heian Shrine precincts.

GION FESTIVAL (July 16–24)

Gion Festival is one of the three largest festivals in Japan. The highlight of this festival is the procession of 29 floats of various shapes and designs on the 17th and 24th.

DAIMONJI BONFIRE (Aug. 16)

This is known as Daimonji-Okuribi. A huge bonfire in the shape of the Japanese character " 大 " (Dai) is lighted near the summit of Mt. Nyoigatake. Other shapes are lighted one after the other on five hills around the city.

FESTIVAL OF AGES (Oct. 22)

The main event of this festival is the procession of some 2,000 people dressed in costumes of important epochs from the latter part of the eighth century to the 19th century, during which time Kyoto was the capital of Japan. The procession starts from the Old Imperial Palace and ends at the Heian Shrine.

KURAMA-NO-HIMATSURI (Oct. 22)

On the night of October 22nd, the villages of Kurama build large bonfires in the middle of the roads leading up to a shrine on Mt. Kurama in Kyoto North. The area seems alive with the brilliant light of hundreds of torches.

Kyoto's Subway

The city of Kyoto is promoting the construction of subways as a basic solution to the municipal traffic problems. Its No.1 Line known as the Karasuma Line opened on May 29, 1981. This line runs from Kyoto Station to Kitaôji under Karasuma Street (see photo on p.97). Additional lines are in the planning stages to provide a new means of transportation for citizens and visitors with the five purposes of volume, safety, speed, comfort, and precision kept constantly in mind.

HOIKUSHA COLOR BOOKS

ENGLISH EDITIONS

Book Size 4″×6″

COLORED ILLUSTRATIONS FOR NATURALISTS

Text in Japanese, with index in Latin or English.

First Issues (Book Size 6″ × 8″)

1. BUTTERFLIES of JAPAN
2. INSECTS of JAPAN vol.1
3. INSECTS of JAPAN vol.2
4. SHELLS of JAPAN vol.1
5. FISHES of JAPAN vol.1
6. BIRDS of JAPAN
7. MAMMALS of JAPAN
8. SEA SHORE ANIMALS of JAPAN
9. GARDEN FLOWERS vol.1
10. GARDEN FLOWERS vol.2
11. ROSES and ORCHIDS
12. ALPINE FLORA of JAPAN vol.1
13. ROCKS
14. ECONOMIC MINERALS
15. HERBACEOUS PLANTS of JAPAN vol.1
16. HERBACEOUS PLANTS of JAPAN vol.2
17. HERBACEOUS PLANTS of JAPAN vol.3
18. SEAWEEDS of JAPAN
19. TREES and SHRUBS of JAPAN
20. EXOTIC AQUARIUM FISHES vol.1

21. MOTHS of JAPAN vol.1
22. MOTHS of JAPAN vol.2
23. FUNGI of JAPAN vol.1
24. PTERIDOPHYTA of JAPAN
25. SHELLS of JAPAN vol.2
26. FISHES of JAPAN vol.2
27. EXOTIC AQUARIUM FISHES vol.2
28. ALPINE FLORA of JAPAN vol.2
29. FRUITS
30. REPTILES and AMPHIBIANS of JAPAN
31. ECONOMIC MINERALS vol.2
32. FRESHWATER FISHES of JAPAN
33. GARDEN PLANTS of the WORLD vol.1
34. GARDEN PLANTS of the WORLD vol.2
35. GARDEN PLANTS of the WORLD vol.3
36. GARDEN PLANTS of the WORLD vol.4
37. GARDEN PLANTS of the WORLD vol.5
38. THE FRESHWATER PLANKTON of JAPAN
39. MEDICINAL PLANTS of JAPAN

\<ENGLISH EDITIONS\>

SHELLS
OF
THE
WESTERN
PACIFIC
IN
COLOR

Book Size 7″×10″

⟨vol. I⟩ by Tetsuaki Kira
(304 pages, 72 in color)
⟨vol. II⟩ by Tadashige Habe
(304 pages, 66 in color)

FISHES
OF
JAPAN
IN
COLOR

Book Size 7″×10″

by Toshiji Kamohara
(210 pages, 64 in color)